PLANES FLYING OVER

PLANES FLYING OVER

ROBERT ETTY

Printed by imprintdigital
Upton Pyne, Exeter
www.digital.imprint.co.uk

Typesetting and cover design by narrator
www.narrator.me.uk
info@narrator.me.uk
033 022 300 39

Published by Shoestring Press
19 Devonshire Avenue, Beeston, Nottingham, NG9 1BS
(0115) 925 1827
www.shoestringpress.co.uk

First published 2020

ISBN 978-1-912524-70-9

ACKNOWLEDGEMENTS

Acknowledgements are due to the editors of the following publications, in which some of these poems first appeared:

Brittle Star
Dream Catcher
The Frogmore Papers
The High Window
Ink, Sweat & Tears
London Grip
The North
Obsessed With Pipework
The Poetry Village
South

CONTENTS

1

UNLIKELY WEATHER ON THE MARSH IN MARCH

For what it's worth, the first day was Wednesday.
At noon, having climbed without looking down,
the temperature passed the twenty mark.
Not-out-yet leaves twitched and stretched in surprise,
mud steamed and dried to an August-type ochre,
blue sky balanced on Somercotes spire,
and March faced an identity crisis.

Out at the school, doors and windows were open,
red-fleshed children in half-buttoned shirts
filled bottles at taps and spattered each other,
while teaching assistants were checking
their watches and saying it felt like Sports Day.
This was still happening in lesson time,
but Mrs West didn't bother to whistle.

Afternoon sprawled in its own heavy heat,
and the day's whole point was forgotten about.
Cows understand every kind of weather
but couldn't explain today. Parents in shorts
met sun-dried kids and rushed them home to the fridge.
Tea should have been salad, dusk should have lasted
till ten to ten on a sleepless night,

but this was March, not BST yet,
and the central heating came on at four.
But Thursday turned out to be almost as balmy,
blossom and more buds exploded on Friday,
and people started to rethink their life
in the light of the Saturday sun.
(A poem about Sunday follows below.)

WHILE THE WEATHER

'Stay and sit,' he'd say, 'while the weather takes up.'
We'd sit and look at piled clouds hardly moving,
swifts circling, plums weighing heavy and purpling,
the old black tom cat from the end house asleep,

and drink tea from blue mugs and eat gone-soft biscuits,
and hear someone's motor mower choking,
all while the weather took up.
The weather took everything up, but not yet.

FOUR SENTENCES ABOUT WEATHER AND PIGEONS SOON AFTER DAWN IN JANUARY

This morning's the iciest morning since
the last one that was as icy as this.

A car's skidded into the local lamppost
and hoisted it over Norman's mixed hedge,
which means until now it's been too dark
to investigate why the lamp wasn't on
and which parts of itself the car left behind
when it slipped off the scene without them.

A curtain of cloud's letting light underneath
(like a roller blind more than a curtain),
and frost on the field turns to pink, almost rose,
as sky dabs and powders its face for the day.

Four wood pigeons trust in a willow branch,
grey-membraned eyes taking eight dim views,
and unmoving except to shuffle along
an approximate pigeon's-width apart,
with nothing in mind to coo to each other
on subjects they usually coo about
in the cooing season, when life's worth seeing
and pigeons feel pleased to be pigeons, perhaps,
but perhaps being a pigeon is always enough.

ON THIS SITE
on June 16th 1452
Nothing Happened

If it weren't for this plaque on the terraced house front
of 77 Sixhills Road, no one
would be aware. So many things happen
everywhere it's refreshing to learn that
here nothing did. It depends on what didn't
happen, though: clearly there wasn't an Earth's Core-
deep earthquake, no slaughter of armed bandits
stealing manure, no plague of gannets
or athlete's foot, no well water turning
to liquefied madness, or old women
giving birth to otters. Then again,
nothing else either.

75 and 79 remain rendered
and plaqueless, their days of events and non-
events unimmortalised for eternity.
But 77 stands self-evident
that here was a day when nothing happened:
no rabbits lolloped, no dandelion clock
shook its seeds on a breeze, no light rain
decided to fall a bit later, no
teenage girl kissed a teenage lover,
no labourer lifted a row of potatoes,
no father mourned a son.

On May 27th 2019
the sky's pale blue
with two vapour trails making a Y.
A man on a scaffold's repointing the chimney.
He calls to a man with a dog and some milk,
who laughs and unlocks his car. The cat
on the window sill sneezes and blinks.
A boiler van slows outside, and the driver
checks numbers and moves further down.
It won't be long, and something will happen.

POWERLESS IN TOWN AT HALF-PAST NINE

The pharmacist in her white coat and I
are conducting a £4.99 transaction
when the power's cut off all over town.
With her cash tray exposed in the strange false dusk,
she fumbles me five pound coins and a penny
and tells me how lucky I am.
I'm working this out when a twilit voice calls,
'We're so sorry—would you all leave?'

As far as a shopper's eye can't see,
the rest of the shops are in twilight as well.
Shop assistants decline to assist
and shepherd customers back from their counters,
apologising for being ungracious
as shades of Schadenfreude descend.
Power being granted's taken for granted,
acknowledged only when it won't jump at
the finger snap of a switch or a socket.
Right now, for instance, no one can spend,
and purchasing's the spice of life, that gives it
all its flavour. Tills have ceased chinging,
purses have clamped, and jaws have fallen open.
The power to prevent has wielded itself,
and preventing it wasn't an option.
Life's wired for such possibilities,
but possible's not the same as frequent,
and any unlikelihood's always likely
if no one thinks it is. (The library lends books
on chance and frequency, but its computers
are down.)
In a flash, like a blessing,
disconnections are reconnecting
and power surges in on a rush of current.
Reenergised, we get back to business,
contactlessly, with acceptable PINs,
empowered to overfill baskets and trolleys

or say 'It's nice, but no thank you.'
Power plays, power points and power showers,
so more power once more to everyone's elbow,
tappable into omnipotently.
The balance of power has tipped in our favour,
but storing an elbowsworth might make sense,
in the light of the chance of a lights-out.

A DAWN CHORUS HEARD FROM A BUDGET HOTEL VERY CLOSE TO THE A34

On the Quiet Floor in Room 200
the standby light, which has stood by all night
in televisual companionship,
dims remotelessly at 4 a.m.
as a new dawn discovers the curtains
don't fit and sidles in at the edges.

The first to dawn call is a tweeting lorry
reversing into last night. No, that's
the second: the A34
has never stopped churring, but softly,
so that it comforts the sleepers
and slightly inclines them to give good reviews
when the so-easy Rate-Your-Stay email
requests two minutes this afternoon.

Dawn takes on the challenge of morning,
backed by the local mixed voice choir,
in which sparrows defy their endangeredness
to chirp their precise location,
while starlings mimic the medley of birds
that sang at dawn when milkers grazed here
(or forget to, and click and rattle, grate, squawk
and tswee-oo, and one starling sounds like six).
Accompanying harmonies swell from
the slip road, where vehicles accelerate
up to The SOUTH. Inside on the corridors
doors wheeze and boof, and let footsteps out
and down staircases to where parked cars
react to radio signals
and gear themselves up for subservience
to a sat nav's sense of direction.

Starlings and sparrows complete their announcements
and find that they really must fly. Late
checkers-out clatter keys at Reception
as traffic's million backstories back up
at traffic lights that don't lighten it.
The breakdown now blocking the A34
looks likely to put drivers' nerves to the test.
Morning's finger runs down an agenda
that hasn't been written yet.

THE DAWN CHORUS AFTER THE SHORTEST NIGHT

In a tree on a hill in Powys
a single bird opens this morning's bill
in the running order of dawn choruses
set in dawn air long ago or longer
by singing above the hisses of rain
its testimony that it is a blackbird
and not the song thrush that will soon join in.
    Dawn on the back of each sheep in each field
highlights dyed-in-the-wool genealogical records
and all the latest gestational data
a ewe would otherwise keep to herself.
    The mice in the church might interpret
the songs as commands to do laps of, or leap
off, the altar they've sprinkled with droppings
since last time its cloth and dead flowers were changed.
    Some birds and perhaps the beautiful cat
from Old School House know (or have seen, at least)
that rain's blocked the road with a branch it brought down,
and might eavesdrop on the bath nurse's alarmed call
regretting she'll miss Miss Moss's bath time.
    Across the valley two golden horses
prepare for passing a day on a hillside
by gazing ahead and shaking their manes.

    Morning hears its dawn chorus out
and watches from the wings. The light will be less
than yesterday, so not a second's spare.
The chainsaw man's halfway here in his van,
and Old School House cat's begun mousing.
Most things might happen, and some of them will,
if not in this valley, then somewhere.
The overdue bath nurse phones back to say ten past,
and sheep are bleating sheep observations
on how they see today going.

THE ACORN KIDS HELPER

This is the grass path the Acorn Kids helpers
help the Kids down on these dewy mornings,
mitten in mitten across the graveyard and over
the bridge to the wood they call theirs, to watch
the sawing man on one knee coppicing
hazel and aspen saplings that suffocate
the ash and oaks he wants the light to see.

The Kids, in wellies and Kid-size hi-vis,
are paying attention to being less silly
instead of the wreath of collared dove feathers,
why a cormorant's changing direction,
the paper chain of grazing brown cows,
a crowd of wind turbines waving bye-bye, or
latrines local badgers replenished last night.

The thought might cross the mind of a helper
that one day one of the Kids will stand here
after sixteen years in New Zealand, let's say,
and, glimpsing through elbowing oaks and ash
a cormorant flapping and wind turbines
turning, might sense a kind of lifting of blinds
about what the reasons used to be,

but the jury's out on *used to* and *reasons.*
The second thought crossing her mind, if it does,
as she guides a child between barbed wire
and puddles, might serve to remind her
that coming back anywhere's a reminder
that memories alter for being remembered,
and not to expect a return from the jury.

THE LAND REGISTRATION ACT

If these foxes were to apply, the law
of adverse possession might favour them.
Rain's wiped the records, but generations
have trotted across the long path they've pawed

from a bramble patch to the scrawny spinney,
and watched from safe distances anyone
pausing to watch them across the rolled field,
with ice in ruts squeaking and crows at a loss

and swallows and combine harvesters
wintering between memories and wishes.
Which multinational last purchased this land
most people and foxes couldn't say,

but the likelihood of whoever sealed it
contesting trespass with this weary vixen
mooching windsweptly over wet mud
is as slender as the vixen caring.

Except that the vixen believes (but doesn't)
it's hers because she's here and it is,
with earthworms and mice now the berries are finished.
Or, if not that, it's here and she is.

ASKING FOXES

So many decisions you face in a field
between this hedge and the next, such as
was it a cuckoo or sparrowhawk
that skimmed the hawthorns over your shoulder,
and whether the tree where the ditches meet
is a hornbeam or a beech, and what kind
of thought you'll permit today.
Then which direction to take at the gate,
and circular or there and back
(or neither, because your phone forecasts rain
and these aren't your Gore-Tex boots). And is this
a north wind, or north north-easterly?
Gets down your neck, whichever it is.

Two foxes pad across the rolled land, one
behind the other: which is the vixen
and which is the dog? Countryman 1 says,
'The big 'un's the dog—he must be, for muscle.'
Countryman 2's in the mood to differ:
'The vixen's bigger. She'll be expecting
and eating for six.' Short of catching up
with both foxes and risking offence by staring hard,
or smiling, excusing yourself and asking
a gender-stereotypical question
like 'Which of you puts the carcases out?'
or 'Who's knitting bedsocks out of couch grass?',
it's difficult to be sure.

All these questions with hands in the air,
as if answering them is the answer.
The foxes are fully aware of who's who
but not that it's Tuesday the thirty-first,
unless there's a calendar inside the den,
in which case, who hammers the nail in the wall?

WORK PARTY,
or WHEN DAYLIGHT'S LET IN

The job that frosty morning was simple:
walk down the ride at the side of the wood
and find piles of saplings we'd coppiced
last autumn, drag some back among older trees

and lose them in there where brambles would grow,
and build a fire and burn the rest. No more
than about three hours' work, Richard said,
and he'd stay behind and watch the fire die.

He didn't say we might notice
each time we pulled a sapling out of the pile
and hauled its thin length across the mud
new pink buds in clusters spaced along it,

quite coarse on a gloveless hand or wrist,
that all the saplings were sprouting as if
they hadn't been sawn through a foot from the ground,
and because a tree buds in spring anyway.

AFTER TURNING OUT THE BEDSIDE LAMP, 7th MAY 2019

Something today
          worth being there to know:
a place where
          early purple orchids grow.

PAUSING TO WORRY IN A SPINNEY NEAR ALFORD

Late this September afternoon
there's nothing downhill you mightn't expect,
only fences, wood pigeons, brown cows, rolled fields
and several part-houses aspiring to wholeness.

In here's a felled oak, ash veined with ivy,
a love heart still growing ring by ring
and a ditch hibernating for summer.
A dragonfly dragonflies backward

and forward, whirring into green light and out.
This is where nature rehearses enduring
and labourers fall sadly short.
When a wren alarm-calls, the spinney's alarmed.

Dragonflies fly (without knowing how long)
for a measure of weeks or months.
Measured in spinneys, worries weigh differently.
Measured in dragonflies, different again.

SAME CONNECTION

On the shadowy side of the hedge, where
dandelions seed like an endangered species,
badgers ignore social distancing guidelines
that country walkers on this side keep to,

except where the footpath's so over-bushy
their elbows might brush, and they duck through a gap
to the set-aside and tread narrowly
where badgers engaged in starlit business

have parted the grass to the spinney and past.
The footpath follows a less winding route,
but badgers' means and ends might well be
as judicious as the rumoured priest's

who at some time during the last millennium
wore the path to link his poor churches—
unless the badgers preceded him,
in their way of knowing what was required.

JOHN DEERE AND NEW HOLLAND

Little moves in these wide, flat fields (as far
as a human eye can see) between
any minute and the next: two swallows
swing low over primrosy ditch banks,

two cantering dogs leave their walker whistling,
a skylark spirals down its song
and, one in a field on each side of the hedge,
two tractors turn their backs on each other.

A John Deere, its green the green of the wheat,
tows a disc plough to the end of the line,
reverses neatly and combs a route back
to where the land dips behind itself.

The New Holland, blue against the beige soil,
with red sprayers held out like dragonfly wings,
covers its tracks with a pesticide screen
that hangs and thins half a furlong further.

A non-human eye might see more than this,
or, if not more, then other. Deer and owls
view panoramas. A buzzard will spot
a rabbit's scut a parish boundary off

and snails keep an eye out for darkness.
Eye-level alters proportion, and proportion
alters degree. Two distant tractors turn
to dust as leaves multiply into trees.

2

A SHORT DREAM WITH A KETTLE

It hadn't been clever to drive the whole way
to my grandparents' cottage (the one that blew down)
via Brigsley and Ashby-cum-Fenby back lane
with a plastic jug kettle in my hand,
but by five I'd arrived. This felt like the close
of a hot summer day, but they'd lit the stove,
and crisp fallen leaves were waltzing around,
unless they were weasels. I rushed to the stairs
and was halfway up when my dad emerged
from a gap in the landing, licking ice cream
with a full head of hair (my dad, not
the ice cream), as if he'd known all along.
Searching for an unoccupied socket,
I found that where the fourth wall ought to be
was a holey hedge dotted with rose hips
and budgies, through which in the sinking salmon
sunset Dirt Walters's house looked exactly
the same as when Dirt Walters lived there,
when Steven whose wife left him weeping in it
was being a small boy in Spalding. Then
bronze mists descended, like not especially
special effects, and Mrs Gray's white house
bronzed mistily. The consequences
were too dreamlike to follow, but sometimes
a dream replays and develops, which sometimes
unravels how it began for the dreamer
who mulls it over at breakfast.

All this knocked another nail in the coffin
a joiner has sawn and sanded and planed
in the shavings-floored workshop that's waiting
its turn to backdrop a future dream.
The trusted website *Dreams and Their Meanings*

lists nothing specific on driving with kettles,
which leaves me a bit in the dark for now,
but it helps with Gandhi, navels and Velcro,
should any of those appear tonight,
which, now I've referred to them, they might.

THE BONES

Since no one's left to pad out the story,
these are the bones of it: Saturday evening,
an RAF base (south Yorkshire, most likely),
the last weeks of World War Two.
The lads fix to meet at a hotel in town—
they might not be here next Saturday night.
The bar soon fills, and there's laughing and noise.
The girls are friendly. They all should be dancing,
but where's the band? The barman says the band's
gone to War, but they didn't take the piano.
As far as the airmen know, no one can play,
but somebody calls out: 'Who plays piano?
Let's have some music!' And tall, quiet George says,
'I play a bit', and they slap his shoulders
and let him through, and he plays a bit for hours.
They sing and dance because War's nearly
over, and here come the post-War days.
Lads line up pints on the piano top,
too much beer by half for one pianist,
and anyway George is no drinker.
Then someone announces they ought to lock up,
and George is shutting the piano lid
when one of the men leans across and says,
'By, bloody hell, George, though, you're a dark horse!
All this bloody time, and none of us knew.'

This is quite slender, as stories go,
but it has a beginning and moves
to an end, with a crisis in-between.
There's still some fleshing out to be done,
which bare bones leave plenty of space for:
uniforms, Brylcreem, blue smoke in glass light shades,
the shade of the lipstick the girls lay their hands on.

And how have they got there? Bikes? A lorry?
Will any man marry his dancing girl,
or only promise to?

What do the old ones
keep to themselves as they watch from the side?
Possibly stories with broken bones
they could relay the flesh onto if they wished,
but old ones don't tell all that might be told.
Or if they do, not the same way twice.

LOST PROPERLY

It was only a scarf, and I have some more.
Slate grey, with paler grey lines in a check,
but not in check enough. A scarf wouldn't
matter much normally, but this was tied up
in generations. It features on two small
black and white photos, warming significant necks.
The necks are gone too, which couldn't be helped,
but the scarf was a picture of health.

In the way things turn up, and out, and
corners, it shouldn't have been hard to find.
But it wasn't in the wardrobe, on hooks, in cupboards,
the car boot, on floors. I emailed a café
(which had it, but didn't), and called back at shops,
the library, the dentist's. Searched the house again,
and the shed, and the car, then a long-shot shop,
thinking why not wear one of the others.

It must have been lost too well to be found.
You unwind a scarf without noticing,
don't you, and drape it over the chair behind,
push it a quarter-depth into a pocket
or hang it where you'll forget you've been.
Today's blue scarf witnessed Grimsby v Tranmere,
kept the rain out and saw me home. So far,
so ok, but look at what went on before.

EVER

In the infants' school with the field around it
'ever' was a daily word, repeated together,
but never thought about or explained:
ever, and ever, and ever, and ever,
and ever, and ever, and ever. Amen.

Sun beamed in through the ceiling-high windows
that Mrs Plant with the light blue hair
pulled open with a gold hook on a pole,
and 'ever' seemed something to do with the sun
and the field that you couldn't see to the ends of

where combine harvesters blew bits of straw
through the criss-cross fence in the summer term,
and no one would ever go far from here
except Lena Nowak who went to Glossop,
and no one had ever heard of Glossop.

'Ever' had something to do, as well,
with Anthony, who lived down the road
in a house on its own with chickens and ditches,
and who (they said) had a poorly heart,
so he didn't come to school every day.

And with closing your eyes in the biggest room.
And a green hill far away.

THE EARTH'S CRUST

When temperatures climbed to 80 or 90
(the figure was always Fahrenheit),
and adults were clearly too hot to be bothered
to ask was it hot enough for us,

the steamrollered tarmac on our narrow road
erupted in oozing pockmarks and scabs,
and smells of moist blackness escaped and hung
in the unmoving air, and we breathed them in

but never quite out, as if one unimaginable
day we'd want to be reminded.
The tyres of vans and cars and the dust cart
rolled slowly and stickily over the tarmac

and plucked it in clusters of glossy crumbs
that didn't fall back but left wider abrasions
than the spontaneous bursts had made, and then
rolled on their way, printing fresh black zigzags.

Summer tar was too hot to handle
and came with emergency heatwave measures
involving avoiding smeared shirts, skirts or plimsolls.
Heat hazes outside Mrs Newton's hedge

and up on the Wall's ice lolly shop corner
foreshortened the world for an afternoon,
and the road our houses were built along
might completely cave in before back-to-school week.

PLANES FLYING OVER

In my aircraft phase I'd lie on my back
in the neighbours' dandeliony grass
(we shared a path between our gardens)
and scour skies the blues of Humbrol paint lids
for the floating delta or quick, silver cross
of a Meteor, Javelin, Canberra, Lightning,
any V-bomber or anything else
on the flightpath to or from RAF Binbrook,
which even by country bus wasn't far.

Often in summer after a meal
my dad would come down without his jacket,
bringing some stale crust or bacon rind,
and sit on the bench against the nest box
and watch his black hens in the run. He'd say,
'Never mind aeroplanes—chuck some bread in!'
and break me a piece to slot through the wire,
and the hens would scuttle over and peck it,
fling it into the air and bicker.
I'd lean beside him and feel his warm shirt
and join in watching the hens. When they'd gulped down
the bread or rind, they'd go back to scratting
at the bald earth, scraping for worms or shoots
that weren't there, stabbing between their claws.

Their squawks, clucks and warbles explained, if we
listened, the pointlessness of searching again,
and apologised, but they couldn't help it.
I'm listening now, and they're still explaining
how these days you need to keep doing and trying
because if you stop there'll be nothing.
There they are, under a wide sky near Binbrook,
scratting the same few square yards.

SEASIDE STORY,
or IMAGINING DONKEYS

Cleethorpes was teeming because of the heat,
so I had to queue for my donkey ride.
The boy in front of me looked about 4
and the girls in *Frozen* T-shirts 8-ish.
I've looked 70-plus ever since I passed 60
(put it down to baldness and wrinkles),
so I asked for an over-12s ticket, please,
and a considerate donkey. Madonna (who was
quite broad, as well) displayed no age concerns
to speak of, and she and I trekked after Paige,
her minder, who seemed unable to hear
my questions on donkey matters generally,
so I composed myself, tall in the saddle,
with both sandals spooning the sand.

The Humber glistened in tints of brown,
and children swashed in its shallows.
The mid-blue sky made gulls all the whiter,
Spurn lighthouse thumbs-upped on its distant spit,
and tankers quivered in the heat haze.
Madonna's ears flicked the fun-loving flies
that tagged along to the turnaround pole,
and the Pier jogged in step with us
down the homestretch. The boy who looked 4
won by a short head, and his dad hauled him off
Ronaldo's saddle with sunglazed glances
in my direction, as if I ought to know better.
I fondled Madonna's tasselled ear
and wished her the best life can bring.
Then I treated myself to a chocolate waffle
and drove home down North Sea Lane.

Apart from the odd anachronism,
the story's more or less factual.
It goes without saying the Humber was brown,
and children were splashing and whooping.
How hot the day was, gulls, tankers, everything
happened like that. The main difference is
I was 5 years old, and my hair looked better,
and it was my dad hauling me. Madonna's
a name for the modern donkey, but donkey-
jockeying skills are the same, like the smells,
shouts and screeches, burnt shoulders, and things
you didn't dream you'd remember instead
of others you thought you would. Much hasn't
changed, give or take some growing. Time's
a cheetah, age is a has-been, the Humber's
a blend of the Trent and the Ouse.
Aching-backed donkeys put out to grass
suffer aching flashbacks of Cleethorpes beach,
and 70-plus-looking people imagine
once waving goodbye to a waving tide
from the upper deck of a blue and cream bus.
Imagining helps to make sense of what happens.
Imagine the donkeys all looking round
to see the same bus turn the Wimpy Bar
corner and nodding in the way donkeys nod
at any sense there is to be made
as the lighthouse fades in the fading light.

SNOW FIELD

First Field, which usually came a poor second,
rose to first choice in the snow. We slid
in the tyre tracks of dilly wagons juddering down
to the sewage farm that stank across half
the village in August, but now the air
smelt of cold. First Field whitened into an ocean
to wade in, to kick, to chuck, to roll boulders
out of, lick lumps of, piss yellow holes in, think
marvellous and offer up bones to for chilling.

The trek to Infants' School in winter
imprinted an image of other white
spaces fringed with lengths of lacework hedges,
and kids who'd suffer from chilblains at bedtime
slinging snowballs that drew blood from cheeks.
Then doors were unbolted at either end,
and bleeding-cheeked kids with dormant chilblains,
who hadn't realised how numb their feet were,
slithered inside and peeled off sodden mittens.

Snow covers tracks and lays groundwork for more,
but the pre-spring clean sheet spread across First Field
finally withdrew its Big Fresh Start deal,
and soon cows and cowpats and cowslips moved in
out of force of habit (which could be the force
that sharpens the memory up to the point
where snow falls at the drop of a bobble
hat, and where there's a place that's untrodden still
if you're one step ahead of a thaw).

LONG SHORT DAYS

When afternoon grew tired of itself,
and Catherine announced that today felt to her
like January the seventy-fifth
instead of only the twentieth,

an email dropped in from Michael in Yorkshire
saying that after his early appointment
he'd walked to the beach and home through the park,
and morning at that time was wonderful,

and he wrote that the weather forecasts
wouldn't affect his plans for Monday,
and that it's important to make the best,
and yet you don't, do you, in some of the months.

THE HAILSTORM PART OF IT

Childhood amnesia being what it is, you've probably
forgotten now the Easter Monday on Turnpike Road
when a cloudful of hail took aim and fired
and your pushchair hood ballooned or blew flat, and hail
stung your cheeks and your hands, and you cried.
If I ran to push you to somewhere safer, the hailstones
hurt you more. If I steered up the grass verge and put
the brake on and tried to shelter you under my arms,
the hail swirled in at you all the same. Any port
in a storm, so I leant half-over and pull-pushed one-
handed, which seemed to be drier than standing still,
or maybe the storm felt the sun at its back and held off,
from a sense of fairness.

Hailstorms like this, with meteorological
explanations, lost their shock value the oftener
they struck. Other versions came cold on their heels,
that weather forecasters failed to forecast, and still
they come, but they aren't the point. The point
(unless it's changed in the telling) is tears melting
hailstones on your cheeks, your tangled wet hair,
then a gap

then a kitchen, red and white plates on our table
and the tin of pink wafers that made things better.

DECEMBER 30th, 15.50 APPROXIMATELY

In the aftermath of Christmas Day,
Boxing Day, day after Boxing Day,
aftermaths of dinners and clearing them,
Skype calls and sleeps, of our squelching steps
on other walks, we're walking now in the endingness
these short days feel to have at their heart.
You're in your Christmas checked scarf
and the black coat I think isn't thick enough,
and borrowed, expensive, waterproof boots.

It's sunset, and sky's the gunmetal backcloth
people face up to in East Coast winters,
except for the even band of primrose
a cold finger's height above the firs
that's splashed with crimson-edged, violet duck-prints
across us and fading out of our sight.
Ducks, it's known, are birds to trust: for instance,
their sense of direction. I take it you bore
the direction in mind, and haven't looked back once.

POEM WITH OCCASIONAL BIRDS

A pair of grey wagtails, conspicuously yellow,
met us at ten in Boscastle Harbour,
as if, with tailwagging panache, they'd dropped by
to mark an occasion. They must have been
(not that they called to confirm it) perfecting
a nest in a hole in a bank, to which end

they pincered sprigs in their beaks and flew them
over and back. We had an occasion to mark,
as well—well, it happens occasionally—
and rented a brown-ceilinged house at Trelill
and hired two matching collapsible bikes
for day trips to memorable harbours.

But that was then. This will be then soon,
this nondescript anniversary morning
(of something else, but let's not split hairs)
as two wagtails arrive with explosive calls
and flit under the bridge on this unsailed canal
and reduce all the wagtails we've ever seen

to an incomprehension (collective
noun) that still hasn't paused to explain itself.
Sometimes a bird (but no likelier than not)
flies across a moment and pins it,
coinciding with what's being said,
that would only be said then and there:

by coincidence, and this long hedge,
a merlin's flying now, unless it's a sparrowhawk—
James the Birder, who'd tell me for certain,
is probably asleep on a ship in Antarctica,
several weeks into the albatross survey
he undertook on Valentine's Day—

which leads this line back to Boscastle Harbour,
two twitching grey wagtails, some airborne words,
and birds appearing in replication
to people they fly round and over and past,
whose minds occasions might cross at times,
in the unlikely way of it.

NEXT MAY

The folding garden furniture we've kept outside
since May's back in the loft. Please note:
the legs on both the table and chairs
can close like scissors and nip your fingers,
so I've tied them tightly with binder twine.
The sleeve nuts, four bolts and the Allen keys
are in a self-seal bag in the drawer.
The flowery cover's also in the loft,
washed clean. (Well, maybe not what you'd call clean.)

This won't apply till May next year. I mean,
I'll clearly be around to set it up,
but you might want to start if I've gone out.
The other things you'll do better than I would.
It's just I was thinking about your hands.

TWO MILES TO BURFORD

i.m. Laurie Griffin (1951–2017)

Then, after sandwiches on that same seat
and saying this was where we sat last time,
and watching swallows dipping in the heat
above the pond, and hearing one more chime

than we'd expected, we zipped bags and stood,
and took the path that (we remembered) lost
its way inside the churchyard but would
take us, more or less, toward the gateless post

that marked the cottage boundary behind,
and into bright June sunshine after shade.
Past there a roadside meadow garden turned
the corner, all its summeriness displayed

a swaying acre wide to anyone
who walked there through wheat fields on that long track:
vetch, buttercups and cranesbill, red campion,
ox-eye daisies that come back, and back, and back.

WHITE TABLE,
or UNCERTAIN ON PUTIKI ROAD IN DECEMBER

Expecting the email didn't diminish
the difference its first sentence made.
With afternoon hotter even than lunchtime,
I pulled on a sun hat, said, 'Back before long',
walked out to the path, changed my mind
when I reached it, and turned down to Anzac Bay.
The tide was in, but the boats barely shrugged
and a kingfisher didn't fly from its rope.
Up at the garage a shoeless mechanic
wiped his brow with a spanner. Not sure

if I'd intended to, I passed the houseboats
and followed the Causeway's unshaded course
beside mangrove swamps. On Putiki Road,
past Pure Fruit and Veges, heat seemed to ease
itself up a notch, while sub-zero night
half a planet away waved a hand
through the stars to its missing, missed ones.
But aftereffects were losing patience,
which meant something ought to be done, or said,
or thought, or emailed (where there was Wi-Fi).

On Saturday I'd sat outside The Milk Shed,
a few yards along the bank by the road,
with carrot cake, tea and hardly a thought
in the sun at a blistered white table,
and if Emily hadn't called from the doorway,
'Sorry—we've shut', I'd have asked her for tea
at that table again, and things out of place
could have repositioned and fallen back
gradually in. But cafés close (it's a fact
of life), and Emily pulled down the blinds.

The heat lasted weeks. Rain gave up trying,
water ran short, and the tankers ran
round in circles. The Milk Shed opened
four days a week from ten till the pastries had gone.
Occasionally the white table was free,
and I stopped by for tea several times.
It might be free now, with sun gleaming on it,
as snow crosses England on this Sunday night,
which shows in a way how things are different,
which everyone knows, but knows differently.

THE SIGN FOR KOTUKUTUKU NATIVE WETLAND RESERVE

With both hands supporting one hefty end
of the length of kotukutuku we're lugging,
I can't photograph it being removed
from the dense valley side where it's grown. It slips
in our grasps as rain that's breaking the drought
swamps the path and tipples in fits
and starts from long leaves. The duck pond
is keeping its eels a secret,
and fantails are flying too close for their comfort
to feed on the gnats we've set hovering.

When it's dried through, de-barked, shaped and planed,
and *Kotukutuku*'s been chiselled across it,
this piece of wood will return as a sign
declaring the place that it marks shares its name.
This humping out today goes unwitnessed
(unless by the fantails, peripherally,
and the sodden green morning in general),
but what's happening is nevertheless a truth
for time to abide by, after time's fashion,
and after some artwork and groundwork.

If photos are no more than leaps of faith,
the lack of them now doesn't matter:
letters are lining up to be carved
into wood that isn't rectangular yet,
but later will make its position clear
to drivers who come to Kotukutuku
down the steep zigzags between the pines,
let the engine run and prop open the gate
and stand in the grass a moment to read
the words on a sign off the unbeaten track.

A POHUTUKAWA IN-BETWEEN

That dawn, you didn't see me at first
as you drove the Toyota up the drive
because of the glare, a pohutukawa
and fingerprint smears on the passenger window
you squinted out of at other cars
speeding down for the 6.05 ferry.

I couldn't see you for the sprawls of leaves
reaching over the path, but then, in that
second, through dusty sunlight and gleams
on the windscreen, you looked like the outline
you'd passed the interim growing into
while other things took your attention.

We wouldn't have seen if we'd been staring at them
the small changes taking place. But seeing's
not believing: believing is. That all's
all right, for example. Below the houses
three shades of turquoise were colouring the bay
as we went separate ways together.

3

LATE

Early out of habit and choice, Grace is there
thirty minutes before appointments
in case of everything no one sees coming,

like Sheepgate being blocked by a fire engine
while firemen coaxed a cat from a chimney,
which cost her a detour the other day.

She keeps a low-maintenance house and garden,
begins weekend jobs on the Wednesday before
and stocks her cupboards an item in hand.

She puts washing out before it's light,
puts all the chairs out at Fortnightly Bookworms
and puts several noses out of joint

at Earlybirds Club when she's earlier
than the early birds who organise it.
Half an hour early's early enough

for tidy-ups of emails and lists
before going into wherever she is
with senses honed for efficiency,

and sometimes she fills any gaps in-between
with contemplating gaps themselves, that they
self-generate, and she welcomed them once,

but now they're unfiltered distraction channels
of no benefit to brain or soul,
and she'd rather count change than think about those.

Grace's secret is how late she is.
How love hadn't touched her the day she married,
and when it came she advised it to leave.

How jobs never mattered until she'd resigned.
How little Dad and Mum seemed to know
until she caught up with their ages herself—

but catching up's trickier when you aren't sure
what it was that left you behind.
Lately she's thought she'll start cutting things fine

and exploring gaps as if inside one
she might arrive at what she was late for,
or be on time for the moment she's in.

A WOMAN WALKING

If you see her at all, you see her here,
where daffodils line the long road today
from the pink-pantiled house as far as the pond
in the dip at the end, in bloom again
despite the winds that rattle hedges
and scrape the bare fields. She returns
also, week after week, walking neither
slow nor fast, looking down but ahead,
never stepping aside when a car appears
but keeping a practised distance.

The ghost of the thought of a ghost vanishes:
a ghost might materialise out of a mist
but not with an Aldi bag for life.
This is her time to walk to the village –
the same time as yours to leave it behind
and drive up this road and past the pond
on your way to be where you're going.
Where she's come from you're never aware,
nor whether, it dawned on you one of the weeks,
her destination's actually the village

or the black bush where a buzzard's perched,
the stile to the path to the church that's locked,
the bus stop the bus doesn't stop at now
or a place where she'll pause and turn back.
Before she's ignored you, you steer to the middle,
given that she's no business of yours. In that case
not many people are, and you're no one else's,
except for a few, which means it's a lonely
no one's business, and not surprising
she's walking here with a bag for life on her arm.

DOING THE BANKING IN MID-JULY

'Harvesting's due any minute,' Scott's saying,
'and harvest'll happen, never mind debits.'
It's Monday, with window-shaped sunbeams in Barclays,
eight people queuing, TV with subtitles.

Kate stares at Scott through security glass.
She nudges a mouse and says, 'Tuesday at two',
and can Scott drop in, does he think, to chat?
'I'd give you this afternoon, but Faith's out.'

Barclays Creates Opportunities
and Brings Values to Life Every Day.
Today's opportunity is to learn patience,
just one of the values that banking here brings.

We shift our weight to the foot that's awake
and read about how hot Birmingham is.
'I can if I've not had the call,' Scott replies.
'When that comes, I'm buggered for banking.'

Out in the fields the wheat's heads are nodding,
dew's dry by nine, the trucks are on standby,
but some of the kernels are still chewable
and Scott's economic growth's a concern.

Kate measures the queue without looking and wonders
aloud if Scott could ring later. Time hums
like a bee round a borage flower (that is,
it's pleasant to think so), and we who've been

practising patience practise a little
longer. 'Well, pencil me in, love, but if
the wheat's more gold, or if you smell rain,
you'll know I've got summat urgent to do.

'It's out of my hands, the whole thing,' he shrugs,
and the automatic door lets him out.
Kate beckons across to the next one of us
whose hands the whole thing is out of as well.

THE GOINGS-ON OUTSIDE

Ex-truck driver Douglas is crossing his front lawn
to see what's causing a more tuneful racket
than all the usual thuds and clanks
of vehicles drumming across the potholes

three men painted light blue three weeks ago,
that Wendy next door rings the Council about
when she's fed up enough, but fat lot of difference
complaining makes, she complains, and Douglas agrees.

Douglas has been sensing closings-in, and
-down, and possibly -over. Partly it's due
to a building site foreshortening the distance
he previously marked the lower end of

when peering across his fridge-freezer top
at rooks hustling buzzards off the tall trees
he'd felt sure his last sight on Earth would be,
but people, like rooks and buzzards, need perches,

so (though he'd choose birds to be stuck in a lift with)
Douglas takes the point. But lorries aren't the reason
today—a newish New Holland combine
such as Douglas used to drop gear behind

is on its way out to help with the harvest
the farmers will finish by Sunday, God willing.
It's all in a day's not-at-work for Douglas,
who wouldn't have resigned if not for his heart.

Ex-truck men can't help but notice traffic
torturing its shock absorbers on potholes
that self-widen daily. Life bites your ankles,
Douglas believes: see off the buzzards or lose

your chicks; patch up a pothole and watch it wash out.
He almost thinks sometimes he doesn't care,
but he's here at the roadside putting his mind
to what hasn't been done, and should be.

IN WITH GEOFF

'How in the world are you?' asks Spilsby Geoff
as we meet where two roads that have never gone far
once met and decided to settle down.
I say, 'In the world, on a scale of 15
to 64, about 37,
all points north considered, from soles to pate,
downhill with a following wind. Yourself?'
'In the world, higher than you, give or take
my cough medicine. Out of it—now you're asking!'

It's simpler not to point out that I didn't:
with what's to take in—van, brown cat, the river,
Aldi, a moment to stand next to Geoff and watch—
who wants to ask about out of the world?

Someone like Geoff is the answer to that,
whose mind's a black hole of black hole information,
whose cash goes on Frosties and DVDs,
who photographed Greys abducting two cows
near the sewage farm, whose mother stopped trying,
who dotes on the ghost of a nurse named Giselle.

He nudges his glasses, pokes at his beard
and says, 'Why not pop by? You know where I am.
I've videoed stuff on my iPad you'll like
of some visitors I've been having.'
Sounds out of this world, I don't reply, but
look where Geoff appears to be looking,
at branch-tips threading telegraph wires
and up beyond at gulls gliding through light
and a vapour trail erasing itself

and then Geoff's gone, as if teleported,
the cat's going round in concentric circles,
the river's in a rush, and the van starts.

BEXHILL, FOR INSTANCE

The man with the Japanese girl in blue
who's slicing a *pain au raisin* in half
is saying he's formed an emotional attachment.
'This place is in me—if you know what I mean … '

He's too earnest to mean if she doesn't,
it isn't. She nods in assent, in any case.
He's not asking me, but I'm answering yes,
at this table with tea in a city

I didn't select as the setting
for unforgettableness, any more
than the places anyone visits
and senses no special attachment to.

Maidstone, for instance. Lives are designed
for unattachments in order to keep them
manageable. Attachment to places
like Maidstone because of life-modifiers

that happened there despite or because of
it being Maidstone (or Bexhill, or Chorlton-
cum-Hardy) in multiples of visits made,
a life doesn't have room to accommodate:

the heart and brain couldn't cope. What's happened
here is enough for a person, I'm always
convinced when I come again. How many
roads must you walk up and down before you leave

them behind? Yes, and how many thoughts
can you think in a day before there's a load
on your mind? Yes, but how many isn't exactly
the point. It's more the effect than the number.

I knew what he meant, and she knew as well:
something out there beyond definition
(conveniently, given the time allowed).
He meant dear, special things, in a manner of speaking,

which speaking of seems to diminish.
So don't tell me and I won't tell you.
The answer, my friend, is pastries and tea
in a place that's in you, if you know what I mean.

STILL AT THE HOTEL ON THE MORNING AFTER LUKE AND AMBER'S WEDDING

Breakfast's provided until half-past nine
and guests are required to leave before ten,
which means that doors on the Floral Landings
open at ten to ten or soon after,

and elbows and knees hold them back at angles
while suitcase wheels wobble across the thresholds,
and suits and dresses on hangers are swung
across shoulders and swished down the passage.

Someone's forgotten a pair of stilettos
and reappears from the other staircase,
hurrying too much to watch from the window
September dew steaming on the marquee
and magpies jabbing at scraps on the lawns.

By ten o'clock most of the cars are starting,
but one couple forty years into their marriage
leave Room 20 late because of a bracelet
and see on the landing in front of a curtain
lit by a sunbeam that's new to the scene
a spider at the end of a thread

hanging still

at the height of the eyes of the wife, who points
and asks how was it that everyone passing
passed without snapping the silk.
Her husband has no idea of the answer,
and when they can't help disturbing the air,
the spider gyrates and stills again.

He follows her down the stairs to Reception,
and she drops their key in the slot at the desk.
They drive between potholes up to the road
and stay silent as far as King's Lynn.

There's still a sunbeam across the landing
and still in the sunbeam a spider—
if not, by now, in the wedding hotel
then in one of these houses as the sun climbs.

DANIEL LEAVES

He lies for another two hours
after her breathing thickens to purrs
and he thinks she's gone somewhere else in a dream.
He occupies his mind with considering
how *change* will be different from *same*
until, disturbing neither the duvet nor her,
he slides out and pads to the clothes he's decided
are right for the kind of future he has.
He shuts the front door with the click he's been practising,
presses his key, and his car lights up
as if it's just cottoned on.
His case is packed in the boot with some ham rolls
he parcelled last evening while she rang her sister.
The engine he knows he can trust to run quietly
thrums past lawns and contented houses.
A DIY store glows chilly blue,
and the Renault showroom watchman
watches the traffic lights changing to green for him.
Winter's struggling to turn into spring,
and sleet tinkles over his warming windscreen.
The speed limit ends, and distance comes closer.

The policeman parked at the substation gate
on a moonlit stretch of the A46
is almost conscientious enough
to pull him over and ask what the rush is
and why's he here, as a matter of interest—
but it isn't interesting, so he won't.

Daniel drives for fifty-five minutes:
fifty-five more and he'll reach the M1.
If she wakes now and goes to the toilet,
she'll think he's downstairs rattling his laptop,
preparing for business that's none of hers.
Unless he turns round at the next roundabout,

her bedside alarm will beep on *Snooze*,
and she won't hear him showering or feel the steam,
and tea won't appear at the top of the stairs.
She won't find his bowl unrinsed in the sink
or his car frosted over outside.
As she dresses, she'll try to remember
him mentioning having an early start.
She'll blow-dry her hair and tug a brush through,
and when she starts to piece things together
it won't take her very long. She might laugh
in a sour way. She might shout.
She might look for the note that he didn't leave.
Then she'll write in her mind very nearly
exactly the lines he'd have written to her.

Maybe a woman who's woken at three
in an emperor bed in a house he'll pass
is voicelessly phrasing the Post-It note
she'll post on the microwave door quite soon.
They might meet in a Hertfordshire coffee shop
and pool their money, ignoring the risks,
to renovate a small house in Hertford
and, one Sunday morning across *The Observer*,
he'll gaze at a point past his shirt on the line
and say yes, he knew in his bones.

The lorries on the M1 excite him,
thundering southward, creating the past.
He's sucked at sixty into the slipstream.
Does she feel better or worse, now it's happening?
If things don't alter, they'll stay the same,
as his father liked saying, above his head.
He'd tell the children he doesn't have
it's illegal to turn round on motorways
and, if it weren't, it wouldn't be wise.
There's a Little Chef north of Leighton Buzzard

and he'll keep his foot down until he's there.
In twenty minutes he'll sit inside,
slicing underdone toast and jam into twos
and allowing himself to interpret the traffic
as six lanes of a metaphor,
while voices at tables in front and behind
swell and become unintelligible.

THINKING ABOUT DOCTOR WARSAP

Despite March insisting on staying wintry,
Doctor Warsap's roadside magnolia—
the one his lifespan-related event
prevented him ever seeing so flowery—
has glowed like two hundred milky lightbulbs
for the length of a short course of capsules
at least. Patients patiently queuing with symptoms
used to while away time considering
how Doctor Warsap and his practice
had kept in the pink since Nye Bevan's day,
which felt like a curative in itself.
But as if by appointment the opening hour chimed
when the ailing found Doctor Warsap's nameplate
unscrewed from the plaque on the surgery door.

Decades after I waited my turn
his bursting magnolia's brightening the Wednesday
of anyone with a Wednesday to brighten,
like even the tree surgeons in hi-vis gilets
treating the birch round the corner with chainsaws,
whose parents Doctor Warsap might have
indirectly helped to conceive. Still some
with symptoms (and some without)
pass here in March on their way there or back
and pick up his final repeat prescription.

THE SUN SHINES ON MISS MIKKELSEN

Miss Mikkelsen (whose single prospective Mister
suddenly recalled a distant commitment)
holds queues up practically every day.
Shoppers who know come back ten minutes later
to give her time to mis-slot a wrong card,
or talk herself through what she wrote on the list
that she didn't bring in case she lost it.
She enunciates in foul languages
at drivers pulled up at traffic lights
and jabs at the shape the day's taken so far
with her adjustable walking stick.

If you live here, you don't bat an eyelid
but tend to believe at least one of the stories
most locals can spin a version of,
of her undercover translation role
as a Trans World Airways air hostess,
of chaperoning a princess's daughter,
PA-ing an elderly country-rock star
and finally abandoning everything
for a caravan and Marmite and eggs.

Sun's on the town's red tiles this morning.
The church peregrines are scouting for chick-food.
Miss Mikkelsen's baseball-capped and sockless,
in Adidas pants to fit someone else,
heading for the Post Office. The next thing
to do (but opinions will differ) is
praise whatever it is you praise
for the marvellous chance to see her en route,
and even, for some, to queue behind her
and wait as she fumbles two £2 coins
from inside a mitten she needn't be wearing
and drops one that rolls underneath the pen rack.

THE OUTLOOK

Dempsey's house wasn't fit to live in,
even when Dempsey did. Now there'll be one
in his kitchen garden, two in his orchard, three
in the field, and access across the crew yard.

You might think it's going to mean change for the worse,
when the latest going's been fairly good,
but Dan the Man reckons change never fails,
and Dan's the man paying a man on a digger

to dig holes he's planting small fortunes in.
Soon windows will frame the way the wind blows,
with implications for gains and losses,
coming to terms with terms and conditions

and levelling everything up. Still, a man might
stroll past with a sodden-pawed spaniel,
humming a hymn he's known since school,
and someone happening to hear might hum along.

If sadly you miss him, don't despair:
the scales of the changes will fall from your eyes,
and you'll weigh amounts against quantities
and holes against sums of the parts.

Parts of this poem fall short of the mark,
and the rest of it falls nearby. But
the final full stop will be placed perfectly,
and after that comes the outlook. Look out.

AL THE BARBER

Malcolm from Woodbine Row spent a weekend
cementing his weathered front garden wall.
When birds were roosting he took two steps back
to mark his handiwork out of ten
(which is what it was, even though Al
the barber, who passed, jibed unkindly
he'd broken his trowel and used his tongue).
This would be Whitsun '62, a fine year
for world change in ways historians are still pinning
down, but then looked like flashes in pans.
Well, barber Al did see Cuba coming
but missed how the Rolling flaming Stones
would affect his takings soon enough.
Most people sympathised over that,
saying if there were eye tests for perfect
foresight, there'd be a high failure rate.

Malcolm's wall weathered better than Malcolm.
His house is a model of retro taste now they've
dried the Scandinavia-shaped damp patch
and quarry-tiled his toilet. Al didn't live
to enjoy a renascent indecent-
exposure short-back-and-sides, but he swore
he divined it via his scissors, and millions
of heads have proved him correct. Oh, for the
vision of barbers like old Al, those prophets
in their own top-lit mirrors, who saw a world
in a glob of Brylcreem or watched
a man's life out-receding his hair.
If you read this in 2047,
I think you'll be thinking *Hmm, yes. Goes to show.*
If Al's anywhere, he'll tell you the same.

4

SIX WORDS UPSIDE-DOWN

On the unstamped reverse, a century's stains,
like brownish clouds over a darker brown sea,
and the following printed words:
POST CARD, *VELOX* (quadrilaterally),
PLACE STAMP HERE, CORRESPONDENCE HERE,
NAME AND ADDRESS HERE, MADE IN CANADA.
Then, pencilled edge-to-edge underneath,
Please Give this to Brother Nils.

The photograph shows a group of three:
father and mother, son standing behind
(eighteen-ish, a hand on a shoulder of each).
Left is a barrel, first two staves only,
a pale cloth unfolded on top. They're posing
beside their wooden house wall, the son's white shirt
off-white against it. The parents look fifty,
apart but together, his hands on his thighs,

hers clasped. He's thick-moustached, with a full
head of hair, and wears a jacket, waistcoat
and bow tie. She's in a white smock, her hair
centre-parted, head lower than his
and, like him, looks an impulse away from a smile.
To the right at the back is a wooden gate
in a fence that's keeping nothing outside
but the level, distant horizon.

The postcard requesting its own handing-on
has sailed from South Dakota to Grimsby.
Behind the men is a farm in Norway
and parents and siblings who stayed within reach.
Between them are more than 4,000 miles,
eleven years, at least one third person,
and separation's incompleteness
that closeness might have instilled anyway.

A MENTION OF BITTERSWEET

Or woody nightshade, she says Google says:
solanum dulcamara, blue bindweed,
poisonflower, poisonberry, felonwood,
fellenwort, trailing nightshade, bitter nightshade,
Amara Dulcis.
                    She swipes through photos
of purple flowers and ovoid red berries
that children have to be warned not to eat—
tomatoes', potatoes' and aubergines'
cousin, but maybe they don't keep in touch.

But is she thinking, as afternoon pales,
of a silver car making a three-point turn,
escalators, travelators, wheeling
a suitcase to Gate 28?
                              The lasting
taste's bitter, plain chocolate bitter, and makes
the sweet sweeter while simultaneously
pushing it further behind. The word fits
the context exactly enough, but some days
it's better to mean woody nightshade.

THE NAMING OF COLLEAGUES

But turnover's quick, and you don't always hear,
which means Cindy's Sandie, Marvin's Mark,
and Mr Wallworth's Mr Woolworths,
except to Mark, who calls him Wallworthless.
Sophie's been Sophie since Day 1,
but her partner asks for Silky Fish.
Darryl and Darren are interchangeable,
Dozy Daisy seems to quite like it,
and Morpeth's Morpeth (his name or his source).
Sophie answered Sandie's phone and said
there wasn't a Cindy. Mr Woolworths
has been dissolved. Mark detests Marvin anyway,
and Daz and Daz don't mind.

It works pretty well, given that being lasts a lifetime
but being someone else might be better,
and Saturn's an apple, Virgil's a cyclone,
Skylarks were Buicks, a sally's a bellrope,
Darren's @dazboy, Sophie's @sophbabe, you are
who you are, and several people who pass for one
pooled their ideas and wrote this.

NOTHING NEW IN A&E

'Let's start with your name,' the receptionist says.
'Baddeley. Phil Baddeley,' he tells her, and winces.
'Well, you'll soon feel better,' she says. 'Your name is …?
Oh—sorry!' She smiles and writes it down,
asking Phil if this often happens
and does he get tired of it. Phil says
on and off for about sixty years,
and what he gets tired of is jokers
who think they came up with it first
and he's had a sense of humour bypass.
He's tired of tiredness, if she wants to know.
His twinges feel worse. He looks for a chair.

Above a tank of bright, circuit-trained fish
four televised people in peak condition
gauge the life-changingness of some news.
A boy's on his phone and his mother's on edge.
A voice at a door calls, 'Mr Baddeley?'
Phil goes to discover to what extent.

FIRST MOW OF THE SEASON IN THE FOOTBALLER'S PERFECT

Right, so, what it is, then,
I've asked the lawn mower
some questions today:
I've held it steady between my feet
then I've pulled it up sharp
pushed in its adapter
linked with an extension
and powered it.
Then I've crossed it wide
to the opposite touchline
and what I've done there is
I've co-ordinated the button and handle
which that has like got the formation buzzing
then moved it up front.
Then I've turned it and chased it from end to end
and I've cut inside past three or four bushes
maintained a neat line
in dangerous positions
and cut back outside
with a great piece of skill.
I've nutmegged the rose arch
shadowed the sundial
step-overed some flowers
in set-piece situations
closed down the channels
taken four corners
not got caught offside
and ghosted it into the final third.
Then after that I've consolidated
and kept tight right through some second-half pressure
and mown to the whistle basically.

I’ve looped the cable
wound up the loose ends
and shut up shop
and what I’ve decided is I’m going to
take every mow as it comes.

At the end of the day

at the end of the day

at the end of the day

I go to bed.

GIVEN TIME

With acknowledgements to Thomas L. Martin

You think I believe I understand
what I thought you said, but say you're not sure
I've actually realised that what I was hearing
was not what you meant. Well,
I think you told me you've bought [an item]
to take the place of [something else]. Either that,
or you're planning to. Suzanne is [back at work,
or she's not yet] and still can't accept
it's a fait accompli. Your story

and I parted company during the stage
when my iPad pinged, but I tuned in
at [X]'s quick stay in Scotland, where midges
drove him clean up the wall. Then [gap] and [gap]
and [gap], and the car job, and [somewhere]
planning permission's gone through, then your brother,
and tonsillitis. Consequently
'That's great!' and 'Why not?' might equally well
have been 'Hell's teeth!' and 'Let's just hang fire.'

In any no-blame relationship, no-
blame falls on both sides. I'll shoulder it now
if you hand it over, on condition
we quality-time how long we keep spending
misunderstanding misunderstanding.
Time's a kind of present we're given.
Don't put your pension on who's the donor,
or your entitlement to a full refund
on decades that didn't spot your potential,

but gather ye rosebuds, don't miss the boat,
carpe the day (which is like grass),
chase an illusion while it's there,
do as you wish (if you know what you wish),
since this is a once in eternity chance.
Unless it isn't, and if you don't seize it,
alternatives spring up not far behind.
Still, wasn't it William the midges drove crazy?
My guess is he didn't give Scotland time.

04.30: *SOMETHING NOT UNDERSTOOD*

With acknowledgements to George Herbert, Mark Tully and Radio 4

You'll hear it one night when your radio's tuned to
Radio Alone on a frequency more frequent
than you'd expect at an unsocial hour:
comments, stanzas, observations, pensées
for the day, pensive movements from moving

music selected by a presenter
who steers conscientiously clear of the meaning
of something humankind's mystified by
and has wanted since the dawn of dawns
to define and label the parts of.

Understood things are a shared achievement.
Everyone understands *understood*
and breathes out in thankful recognition
when someone says something like 'You know how … ',
but not understood things deserve a series

of 25-minute radio programmes.
Series 11 number 37
(entitled 'Er … Didn't Quite Get the Drift')
happened to be repeated tonight
and featured decontextualised extracts

from various works in audio art forms,
each exemplary in its unclearness,
and which 99.85%
of Radio Alone's cross-listenership sample
couldn't see wood for trees in before.

In this way *Something Not Understood*
is a gentle means of preparing listeners
for not meeting others even halfway,
for lost threads, missed gists, blindsided irony,
dropped connections, jokes four miles over their head

or beneath it, wrong numbers, bad lines, slow
uptakes, slow answers, no answers, no questions,
no comeback, no lookings, no listenings,
but hopes of communicating on a wavelength
Something Not Understood isn't on.

Listeners switch their radios off
and take some essentials and walk out to meet
in the land of spices, where something
understood ends the prayer and is the prayer
and appears without fail in the schedule.

LATE WATCH

My sixty-year-old, inherited watch
has started stopping in-between times
and self-restarting shamefacedly
as if it's heard that lockdown's unlocking,
all appointments have been reinstated,
and time's in need of keeping again.

Searching online for horologists brings up
Mark Time on the second page. In his opinion
my watch sounds perfect for what I'm describing as 'now'.
Mark says he dispensed with himself yesterday.
He wound up his clocks, wound down his workshop
and posted the following on his website:

Gone to watch shadows crossing walls. It's all
in hand. Trust me.
Mark Time (Yours always)

WITH HIM

With acknowledgements to Ben Darvill, BBC Radio 4

'I've never heard it again, that song,'
he says of a rosefinch he heard when waking
once in a tent by a wall on an island.
'And yet it'll always be with me.'

Much makes no connection, or drifts apart,
but the notes of the bird come with him through
all things, although he doesn't explain.
When all the rest fails, there might still be singing.

SOME FACTS ABOUT FALSE IMPRESSIONISM

To avoid false impressions:
    it isn't the avant-garde reacting
by badly applying unpainterly dabs
    specifically not to resemble poppies

or the dance of light on a dancing girl's dress—
    even if the dabs are badly applied
en plein air en France by torn-trousered vieillards
    with unbarbered beards and untreated ailments—

call it a kind of social trend being
    socially followed by impressionists
who don't engage in dabbing paint badly
    but work instead en plein air and indoors

not on canvases pegged to buffeted easels
    but at the fine art of putting across
what it is they mean, which implies as well as
    semantic exertion that putting

across is incidental, and failure to grasp what
    what's put across means is commoner than colds.
(What does *buffeted easel* mean to
    someone whose easel never has been?

And *badly applied*, applied to a dab,
    might pass for the mot juste, just about,
but not if applied to a dab which wasn't—
    allowing for expert opinion, etc.)

The signs are all there, the words on the page,
    the tableaux set for minds not to meet,
for points to be only half-made or half-taken
    and second chances to spend all day begging,

while people affected every half-hour
    sidle off to ponder whether
a trick was missed, and which one it was.
    Movements like False Impressionism (Faux

Dada, Inaction Painting, Uninstallation)
    take time to be seen in their untrue colours,
but critics seldom have it to spare. Seminal False
    Impressionist works invite queues for selfies,

inspire PhDs and radical novels,
    change hearts, shirts and scenery, and hang
around where false impressions are picked up
    and tucked under arms for later.

FROM YOU TO ME

'Not a line of her writing have I' – Thomas Hardy
'With love from me to you' – Lennon-McCartney

If there's anything that I want,
if there's anything you can do,
it's post me a note in your handwriting.
I don't mean don't send an email as well—
some days I get by on a ping and a prayer—
I mean paper inside an envelope
to land on the doormat one morning.
Write in whatever comes to hand:
a pencil's fine (and the finer it is,
the fewer the shades of grey). Biro might make
a deeper impression, and rollerball blots
where you hesitate. Fountain pen involves
filling and drying, so please don't bother with that.

Not much, when you think, is as personal
as letters a thumb and fingers have shaped
on paper the side of a hand has moved over.
This poem was written in pencil first,
and most of it was rubbed out once at least.
If you'd like the draft, I'll send it along,
with last month's car service date on the back.
If not, it's as clear as print anyway,
and too long already to try to say
that the length isn't really the point.

'GOD, THAT FEEDS THE YOUNG RAVENS,'

the warden says, halfway down the page
and well past midnight, 'will take care of me',
and smiles to try to make inconsequential
the consequences his listeners foresee
with the horror of the doubtful.
Nights of dark thinking have brought him to this,
consolidated by dawn choruses.
At Chapter Hotel on the morning after
he copies a letter for two recipients
and leaves to catch a later train home.

Marguerite, who's not in a novel,
who lost her job when reorganisation
made a far better job of it all, smiles
perhaps much as the warden did, and answers
when asked how she's planning to pay Joseph's
second year university fees, 'The Lord
will provide for Joe, as the Lord chooses',
and heads for the baker's while the bread's fresh
and back to the car park before time runs out,
or the heavens open on this side of town,
which she feels a conviction they will.

Consider the ravens, that they sow not.
And then the warden, considering the trouble
he hears whispers of, that so troubles him.
Consider the bullfinch, cold on the ground,
with the seeds in her bill she was carrying
back for her young. Look at the wren's nest
in the old timbers, moss spilling out now
the four chicks are fledged and chit-chitting
from four yellow beaks in a diamond
at whichever parent it is who flits
all day long with insects to feed them.

With acknowledgements to Anthony Trollope

A SENTENCE IN *ADAM AND EVE AND PINCH ME* BY A E COPPARD

From one of the short stories and from biographical notes on the cover of the Penguin Books first edition (1946)

'At the close of an April day,
chilly and wet, the traveller came
to a country town.' Then Coppard describes
how the man had walked there, the long stone walls,
thatched houses at crossroads and crooks of streams,
loneliness broken by larks and hares.
And he entered an inn, and what happened there
takes fourteen more pages to tell.

The biography says that Coppard
was a housemaid's and a tailor's son,
that he left school at nine to be errand boy
for a maker of trousers in Whitechapel,
and the rumour that he became a navvy
and lived on raw cabbage has no foundation,
but actually he worked as a clerk in Oxford
with time for sprinting professionally.

Who's Who gave his recreation as 'resting',
which Wikipedia updates by adding
that in 1957 he turned to
resting eternally, and includes
a family photo (without him), and influences,
tastes and publications. It mentions
the trousers-maker and Oxford but skips
the navvying and the raw cabbage

because (perhaps) there's still no foundation.
Coppard's words have no foundation either,
except in a closing April day
and a traveller on foot, and in fictional
truths which are founded in telling,
and mean that the day and the traveller
were chilly and wet and coincidental
because the story knows that they were.